200+
games
&fun
activities

Kathryn W. Kizer

New Hope® Publishers

Birmingham, Alabama

New Hope® Publishers
P.O. Box 12065
Birmingham, AL 35202-2065
www.newhopepubl.com

Library of Congress Cataloging-in-Publication Data

Kizer, Kathryn W., 1924-
200+ games and fun activities for teaching preschoolers / by Kathryn W. Kizer
  p. 72 cm.
ISBN 0-936625-70-8: $4.95
1. Educational games.
2. Education, Preschool—Activity programs.
3. Creative activities and seat work.
I. Title. II.
Title: Two hundred plus games and fun activities for teaching preschoolers.
LB140.35.E3K9 1989   371.3'97—dc19   89-3176

Cover design and illustration by Alisa Hyde

ISBN: 0-936625-70-8
N898101 • 0100 • 7.5M4

Contents

Contents

Poems and Fingerplays

Chapter 4

Jack-in-the-Box
Where Is Thumb Man?
Grandmother's Glasses
Touch Your Nose
Merry, Old Merry-Go-Round
The Rain
Little Wind
This Is Mother
Five Little Christmas Trees
Do as I Do
I Can
Over in the Meadow
Two Mother Pigs
Five Little Ducks
Here's a Ball for Baby
Hands on Shoulders
Ten Little Fingers
Here Is a Beehive
Once I Saw a Little Bird
I Could Be an Airplane
Kindness to Animals
Little Robin Red-Breast
May Day
The Squirrel
How They Sleep
Buttons
Catkin
A Kite
Taking Off
The Secret
Falling Snow
Friends
Mr. Nobody
Five Little Squirrels
Growing Up
White Sheep
Long, Long Ago
Good Friend
O, Look at the Moon
The Big Clock

Games for Parties

Chapter 5

Ring Toss
Musical Chairs
Drop the Handkerchief
Bowling
Squirrel and Nut
What Color?
Doggy, Doggy, Where's Your Bone?
Button, Button—Who Has the Button?
Drop the Clothespins
Singing Game
Guess What
A Fun Board
Mother Hen
Sewing Cards
Parachute Fun
Blowing Bubbles
Balloon Toss
Mine Are Gone
Leader of the Group
Viewing Slides
Toy Swap
Butterfly Toss
Roll Under the Bridge
Roll the Ball
Bat the Ball
Cluck! Cluck!
Penny Toss
Story Time
Sock Race
Stoop
Sometimes I'm Tall, Sometimes I'm Small
Over the Water
A Spanish Game
Peanut Hunt
Happy Birthday
Cat, Cat, Catch the Rat
Run for Your Life
Take Away One

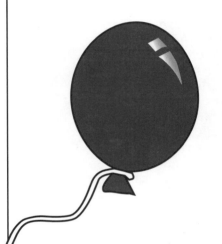

Chapter 1

Games
···· for
Relaxation

Show Us

Instruct the children of various activities to pantomime. All of the children (or one or two) may act out the instructions.
Try some of these:

Show us how you would rake leaves.
Show us how you would shovel snow.
Show us how you would mow the lawn.
Show us how you would pick a precious flower.
Show us how you would hop like a bunny.

Other ideas: stand on one foot, walk like a soldier, walk heel-to-toe on a line on the pavement, hop like a kangaroo, walk like an elephant.

Name The Animal

Choose a person. Whisper the name of an animal in his ear (or let the child whisper the name of the animal in your ear). The child imitates the animal while others try to guess the animal he depicts. Try these: rabbit, giraffe, kangaroo, elephant, cat, pig, cow, turkey, and dog.

Variations: (1) Whisper a community helper for a child to act out (doctor, fire fighter, mail carrier, nurse, check-out clerk at grocery store).

(2) Whisper some way the child can help at home: sweep the floor, set the table, make the bed, mop the floor, run an errand.

Find the Picture

Place five or six pictures in the room. They may be Bible pictures, pictures of a missionary and his work in a certain country, pictures of community helpers, or other categories. Repeat the following poem each time a child is requested to find a picture.

Look quietly and quickly to see
If you find the picture that I see.
When you are asked, bring it to me.

Example: I see a picture of a family reading a book that helps us know how God wants us to live.

Find the Color

Name a color.

The children walk to touch something in the room which is that color. They stand there until another color is named.

Variation: The adult names a color. The children name things that are that color. Example: If brown is named, they could mention potato, shoes, some sunglasses, some cars, etc.

Put Your Hands out Front

The adult says the following instructions; while imitating the motions:

Put your hands out front, put your hands out behind.
Put your hands out front, put your hands out behind.
Put your hands out front, put your hands out behind.
A-n-d
Clap your hands with me.

Put your hands up high, put your hands down low.
Put your hands up high, put your hands down low.
Put your hands up high, put your hands down low.
A-n-d
Turn around with me.

Add other motions. (Put your foot out front, put your foot back behind. A-n-d hop around with me.) Vary the rhythm and speed up the first six lines occasionally. Draw out the *and* to add suspense. Then return to the steady rhythm on the last fine.

Clue

Explain that a clue is like a hint: you tell something about the item without naming it.

Prepare in advance the materials needed for this game by cutting out pictures of animals and mounting each separately on construction paper.

Choose one child to be "It." That child sits in a chair facing the other children. The adult holds a picture of an animal over the child's head and turns it so every child in the group can see it except "It." "It" asks someone in the group to give a clue about the animal (descriptive words or phrases). "It" calls on other children for clues until he can guess the name of the animal.

Variations: (1) Use objects instead of pictures (crayon, paintbrush, paper, chalk, book, puzzle).
(2) Use pictures of community helpers.

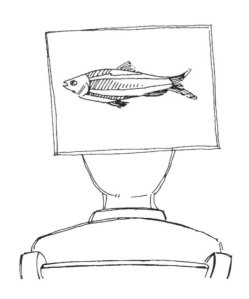

Mirror, Mirror

Talk about what a mirror does, that it gives to you the exact picture of what is in front of it.

An adult assumes a position that the children try to mirror. The adult and children will be face-to-face. Therefore, the children will be mirror images of the adult's position and facial expression.

A child may be the leader for other children to mirror. If children are standing for this game, encourage them to allow enough space for movement and then to stay within that space until the game is finished.

Who Am I?

Say: I'm thinking of someone in this room. He is a boy. You may ask me questions about this boy. You may ask me about his clothes, the color of his hair, and the color of his eyes. You may not ask his name until you know all these things.

The first person who guesses who the boy is may choose someone to be "It."

Taste and Guess

Gather bite-sized pieces of several foods. (Be cautious of allergies.) The child closes his eyes while the adult places a bit of food into the child's mouth. The child tries to identify the food.

Fruits may be used for one experience, and raw vegetables may be used for another. (*Caution:* Avoid carrots because if the carrot is not chewed well, it can cause choking.)

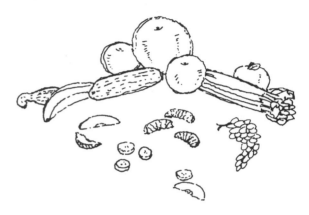

Birds Have Feathers

One child or adult is the leader. The other children flap their arms when the leader names an animal with feathers. They do not wave their arms when the animal does not have feathers.

Example: "Birds have feathers." (Flap, flap) "Ducks have feathers." (Flap, flap) "Dogs have feathers." (Arms down)

Relaxation Game

The following is easy to learn because the words are repetitive. The third instruction is the only one that varies, and you can add anything you like. Enjoy the actions along with the boys and girls.

Stand so straight; stretch so tall;
Turn so slowly, no noise at all.

Stand so straight; stretch so tall;
Touch your toes, no noise at all.

Stand so straight; stretch so tall;
Take a deep breath, no noise at all.

Stand so straight; stretch so tall;
Sit down quietly, no noise at all.

Which Is Bigger?

Explain that if the statement you make is right, the children stand. If what you says is wrong, such as "A chicken is bigger than a cow," the children remain seated and clap.

"A cow is bigger than a chicken." (Stand) "A horse is bigger than a chicken. (Stand) "A frog is bigger than a goat." (Remain seated and clap) "A butterfly is bigger than an eagle." (Remain seated and clap) "A cow is bigger than a kitten." (Stand)

Ask several children to take a turn making one statement.

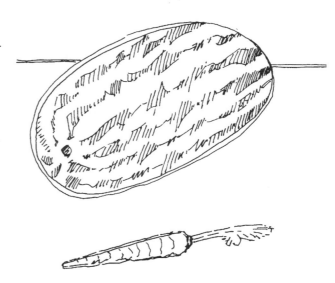

Variation: Foods may be used instead of animals. With young children, however, always stay within the same category.

Examples: "A potato is bigger than a green bean." (Stand) "A carrot is bigger than a watermelon." (Remain seated and clap)

What Are You?

Purchase inexpensive nature stickers, or clip pictures from magazines in certain categories (flowers, birds, animals, or different fruits). Cut 3-by-5 index cards in half, and glue one sticker or picture on each card. Give a card to each child.

Say: If you are an orange, turn around three times. All of you who have flowers, skip around the room.

Play the game several times, giving instructions that include all the cards being held.

Picture Box

Divide the children into two groups. A box containing pictures of animals is located near the children. Ask a child from one group to go to the Picture Box to get a picture. When the child returns to the group, he shows the picture to everyone. All the children in that group imitate the pictured animal. The children in the other group guess the animal they are depicting. Then a child from the other group chooses a picture for that group to demonstrate.

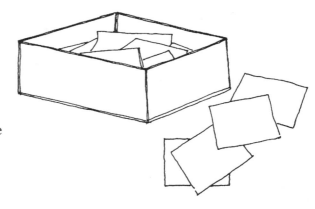

New Friend

This is a favorite game for most preschoolers. Each child chooses a partner. As the adult calls out the following body parts, the partners place together the body parts named: Toe-to-toe, knee-to-knee, elbow-to-elbow, back-to-back, shoulder-to-shoulder, head-to-head.

At any time during the game, the adult may say: New friend. When that command is given, all children change partners.

Variations: Instead of saying *new friend* to change partners, use some other signal. It may be (1) a country *(Mexico, Japan, etc.)*; (2) a community helper *(doctor, nurse, fire fighter,* etc.); (3) or some other word that is appropriate for the study or occasion (such as *Happy Birthday)*.

A Stretching Game

Ask the children to touch imaginary places and things. Say: Touch the sky. Touch the bottom of the ocean. Touch a tall tree. Touch the ground. Touch a big ball. Touch a little flower. Touch the doorknob on the front door. Touch a prickly cactus. Touch a hot cup.

High Stepping Pony

Ask the children to trot around the circle while you chant:

I'm a brown pony that's stepping high;
I'm trotting and trotting as I pass by.

Encourage the boys and girls to lift their knees high as they trot around.

The entire group may be involved in this at one time, several children may be ponies at once, or one child at a time may be selected.

Popcorn

Divide the children into two groups. One group stoops in the center of a circle made by the stooping children of the other group. The boys and girls inside the circle pretend to be popcorn while the other children forming the circle are the popcorn popper.

As the children who are the "popper" begin to rise slowly, the ones in the middle begin to move around, later popping up and down rapidly, just as they think popcorn might do.

Change groups to repeat the action.

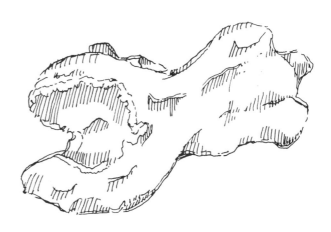

Who Is Knocking?

Children sit in a semicircle. One child sits in a chair with her back facing the group. "It" closes her eyes and holds her hands over them.

The leader points to another child, who tiptoes to knock on the floor behind "It's" chair.

"Who is knocking?" asks the child with closed eyes.

"It is I," answers the child who knocked.

"It" tries to guess who knocked by the sound of the voice. Children take turns being "It."

Follow the Leader

Lead the children to line up behind the leader and to imitate everything the leader does. They walk, hop, skip, jump, skate, stoop over, gallop, etc.

It is wise for an adult to be the leader first until the children are ready to take turns. Play this only for a brief period of relaxation.

Ways to Travel

Briefly discuss (using pictures if possible) different ways to travel, such as by car, boat, airplane, helicopter, horse, bicycle, walking, bus, and canoe. Say: Most of you probably came to church (or kindergarten, or school) in a car or a bus today. Let's pretend that you could come to church any way you wanted to travel. I am pretending I came to church in a _____.

The adult pantomimes a way some people go to church while the children guess. Then let the children take turns pantomiming different ways to go to church.

Changing Chairs for a Purpose

How do you place children in a semicircle in order to get the best attention from each one? Sometimes one or two children will cause difficulties if they are seated next to each other.

This game is a sly way to get the boys and girls seated according to your preferences.

Ask the children to cover their eyes with their hands. Tell them that the two children you tap on the head will change places. When the eyes are opened, they are to guess the two who moved. Of course, this is a quiet game with the leader and children tiptoeing as they move about.

Do not move the ones you desire to separate on the first move. The children will never guess the reason you play this game if you move the children carefully.

Match-Ups

Say: I am going to name an object. When I name one thing, you will name something you usually think of connected with it. See if you can name the object. What do you think of when I say ____?

Use some of the following: salt-pepper; paper-pen (or crayon); lettuce-tomato; spoon-fork (or knife): laugh-cry; table-chair; cup-saucer; dog-cat; shoe-sock.

Spin the Bottle

Cut the top from a plastic bottle. Make the hole large enough to insert slips of paper with a directive printed on each piece of paper. Print some of these to place in the bottle.

- Walk around the chairs, taking baby steps.
- Tiptoe to the door and back.
- Walk backwards to a table and back.
- Hop on one foot.
- Take a friend by the hand, and jump around the room.
- Waddle like a duck.
- Fly around the room like a butterfly.

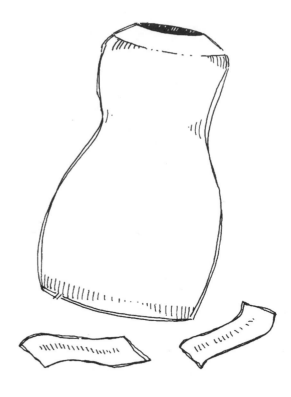

A child spins the bottle, and the one toward whom the bottle points pulls out the instructions for the adult to read. The child follows the instructions. That same child spins the bottle until it points to someone else in the room who takes a turn.

Walk the Line

Using masking tape, mark a long line on the floor. Give instructions for one child at a time to walk the line.

Try some of these:
Walk the line using baby steps.
Walk the line using giant steps.
Walk the line on tiptoes.
Walk on the line backwards.
Skip along the line.
Hop along the line.
Jump along the line.
Run lightly along the line.

Hide and Seek

Choose a child to leave the room with one adult. Hide a familiar object (penny, nut, crayon). When the child returns, explain that when he gets close to the penny (or whatever is hidden) that the group will clap loudly; when he is far away, the group will clap softly.

This game may be played indoors or outside.

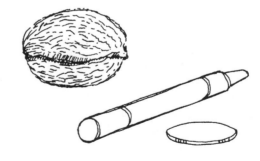

Can You Do What I Do?

The adult chants to the children (or makes up a tune): Can you do what I do?

The children respond in the same chant (or tune): We can do what you do.

Then the children imitate the action of the adult such as touching toes, jumping up and down, touching knees and reaching upward, stooping, and turning around.

Laugh

While seated in a circle, tell the boys and girls that they are to take turns around the circle (one at a time) saying *Ha* without laughing. Each child will add one *Ha* to the one who speaks before he does.

The first player starts by saying, *Ha.* The second player says, *Ha, ha.* Don't worry about the number being accurate as the object of the game is fun and relaxation. Before long, the whole group will be laughing.

Stand up, Sit down

This game is excellent for learning names.

At first, the adult takes a turn before the children have a turn. Say: When I call your name, stand up, please.

Skip around the room until every child is standing. Then say: Now when I call your name, sit down.

At other times, give a preschooler an opportunity to call each person's name and that person stands. Then choose another child to call each one's name to sit down.

Beanbag Games

Toss a beanbag to a child, and ask him to choose the sound of some animal to make for the others to guess the animal. If threes or younger are playing, whisper the name of an animal in the child's ear. Continue until all boys and girls have had a turn.

Variations: (1) Toss a beanbag for preschoolers to act out community helpers, occupations, or to ask the child to answer a review question about the unit of study.

(2) Another game using the beanbag is asking a child to walk while balancing the beanbag on his head, or on his arm or shoulder, etc. Also, he could get down on his hands and knees and walk while balancing the beanbag on his back.

(3) A beanbag toss is an interesting game for preschoolers. Provide a wastepaper basket or can or an open cardboard box for the children to take turns tossing the beanbag into the container.

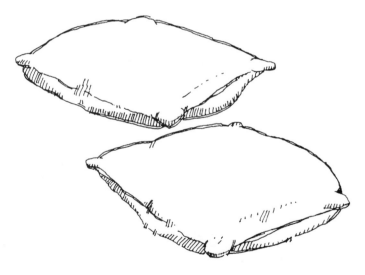

Who Is Missing?

While all eyes are closed and covered with hands, the leader touches one child to hide in a previously designated spot (behind an opened umbrella or screen) where he cannot be seen. When the leader asks, "Who is missing?", the children open their eyes and try to name the child who is away from the group.

Preschoolers enjoy taking turns with this.

Duck, Duck, Goose

The children sit in a circle as one child is "It." "It" walks around the circle touching each child on the head. If she says, "Duck," the child stays seated. If she says, "Goose," the child jumps up and chases "It" around the circle until "It" returns to goose's" chair.

"It" serves another turn if not caught.

Variation: This game may be adapted to units of study. Example: If the study is about community helpers, "It" may name a community helper in touching preschoolers on the head. These children remain seated. If "It" names something or some-one who is not a community helper, that one runs around the circle chasing "It."

Can You Guess?

Select some magazine pictures and categorize them. For example, you may group nature pictures together (not scenes, but primarily one thing in nature) foods, occupations, etc. Use one category for each game.

Example: If you are using food pictures, pin an orange on the back of "It." Ask the other children to give clues (or hints) to help the child guess the food. Boys and girls may give the color of the food, how it tastes, tell that it grows on a tree, or a plant, etc.

Hard Rocks

Ask the children to stoop, curl up into a small ball, face turned downward, to become a hard rock. Say: When I suggest that you become something else, like an animal or an insect, you begin to move like that animal. You may also make sounds. When I say, "hard rocks," you re-turn to the rock shape.

The words you use for giving instructions are: *Hard rocks, hard rocks, act like a _____.*

Include some of these animals in the game: snake, bird, giraffe, elephant, dog, kitten, goat, sheep, and tiger.

Quiet Chair Game

This game is especially appropriate when you want the preschoolers involved and quiet as an adult prepares for another activity.

Place a chair in front of the group. Say: We are going to play the Quiet Chair Game. I will choose the quietest person I see to have the first turn to sit in this special chair.

Wait for the children to get very still and quiet. Select a child to sit in the chair. "It" then looks carefully to select someone who is quiet to have a turn in the chair.

I Spy

Explain that *spy* means *see*.

Say: I spy something that is yellow and green. It is square (book). I spy something that is brown and white. It has four legs (easel).

Lifting and Carrying

Explain that the preschoolers will act out lifting and carrying boxes that are of different sizes and weights. Ask the children to fill their imaginary boxes with cotton balls. Then have them pretend to lift the boxes to carry across the room and back. Repeat this procedure using other suggestions: *Examples:* Fill the boxes with bricks, wood, plastic drinking straws.

Talk about the boxes that are heavy and boxes that are light.

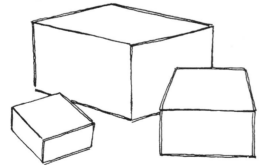

One Clap, Two Claps

Preschoolers are seated in chairs. The adult claps her hands. Explain that one clap is for everyone to stay still in their chairs; two claps are for everyone to quickly change chairs.

Variations: When I name a fruit, clap hands once. When it is not a fruit, clap hands twice.

Stop and Go

Make a red *stop* and a green *go* sign from construction paper. Name an action for the preschoolers to do (jumping in place, jogging in place, tiptoeing, marching). When you hold up the *go* sign, children start moving. When you hold up the *stop* sign, children stop.

Which Color Is Missing?

Place strips of construction paper (blue, green, red, yellow, orange, purple, brown, and black) on a table or floor. Ask the preschoolers to close their eyes and cover them with their hands. While eyes are closed, remove one color. When eyes are opened, preschoolers are to guess which color is missing. Ask the first one who correctly guesses the missing color to name something God made which is that color. Let that child remove the next strip for others to guess.

Variations: This game may be played using (1) several pictures, (2) nature items, or (3) books. (Remember that the younger the child, the fewer items you will show at one time. For the color game, use only four or five colors for twos and threes.)

What's in My Hand?

The adult puts a small object in his hand and closes the hand so that no one can see the object. The child who guesses the correct object takes a turn with another small object. It may be necessary for "It" or the adult to give a few clues about the object. Suggestions for objects are a piece of crayon; a paper clip; a piece of sponge; a cotton ball; a cotton swab; a small pair of scissors; a piece of a puzzle and a small toy.

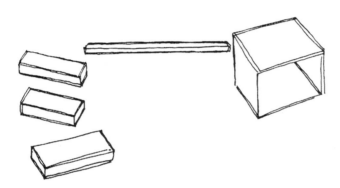

Obstacle Course

For young preschoolers, make an obstacle course including some of these things: walking on a balance beam or on a masking-tape line on the floor; crawling through a tunnel (under a table or through a large cardboard box with both ends cut out); and jumping or crawling over cardboard blocks (not stacked). Encourage the children to go through the course at their own speed as they are not competing with each other.

Keep It Under Your Hat

Hide a small object under a hat while the boys and girls have their eyes closed. Give several clues about what is hidden under the hat for the children to guess what it is.

As the children learn to describe objects, they can take turns hiding the objects and giving clues for others to guess.

Things God Makes

Say: I'm thinking of something God makes. I will give you some hints. Then you guess what it is.

Use simple clues, such as I'm thinking of a fruit. It is long and yellow. God makes it grow. What is it?

The child who guesses correctly takes the next turn.

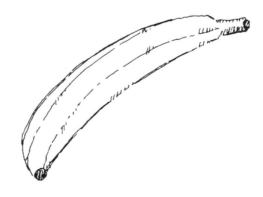

Which Church Helper Am I?

Describe a church helper and ask the children to guess who it is. For example, say: I help the pastor. I sort his mail. I type his letters. Which church helper am I?

Continue playing describing other church helpers.

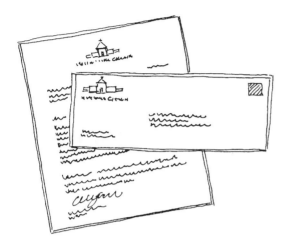

Pretend and Stretch

Guide the preschoolers to pretend to be different things that stretch and move.

Say: Let's pretend to be a tall tree blowing in the wind. (Children stand on tiptoe, hold hands above their heads, and wave from side to side.)

Say: Let's pretend to be a short bush. (Children move to a squatting position.)

Say: Let's pretend to be a frog. (Children leap around the room.)

Say: Let's pretend to be a rabbit. (Children hop.)

After preschoolers understand the game, choose a child to give instructions.

Change Chairs

The adult begins the game by saying: I have a friend. His name is Michael. I want to change chairs with Michael.

The adult and Michael exchange chairs. Then Michael chooses a friend with whom to change chairs.

Where Am I?

Blindfold one child. Ask another child to turn him around, and then lead "It" to one of activity areas of the room. Ask the child to feel the surroundings around him. Can "It" tell what section of the room he is in? Remove the blindfold for the child to see if he guessed correctly. "It" chooses someone else to be "It." The child leading "It" also chooses someone to take her place.

My Chair and Me

First be sure the chairs are far enough apart for preschoolers to move around them. Give directions for the preschoolers to follow, such as:

Stand in front of your chair.
Stand behind your chair.
Walk around your chair.
Pick up your chair.
Touch your chair.
Stand beside your chair.
Put your hand under your chair.
Sit down in your chair.

Hot Potato

To make a soft ball, tie a knot in a clean cloth, man's handkerchief, or nylon stocking. Pretend it is a "hot potato."

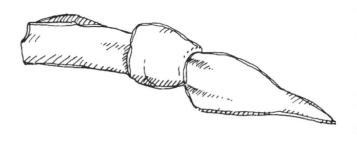

The children sit in a circle on the floor, spreading their feet out in front of them, with each touching the feet of the child next on either side. As the "ball" is tossed to a preschooler, that child quickly tosses it to someone else. Remind the children that they are to handle it as a "hot potato."

One, Two, Three, Change

Inform the preschoolers that there are two rules for this game. First, you must move to a different chair when the leader says, "Change chairs." Second, you cannot bump into anyone.

Count slowly: one, two, three.

Clap your hands once and say: Change chairs.

Do This—Do That

When the leader says, "Do this," the children are to follow the action of the leader. When the leader says, "Do that," the children stand still, even though the leader may try to trick them.

After the children become familiar with the game, let some of the children take turns being the leader.

Chapter 2

Learning
Games

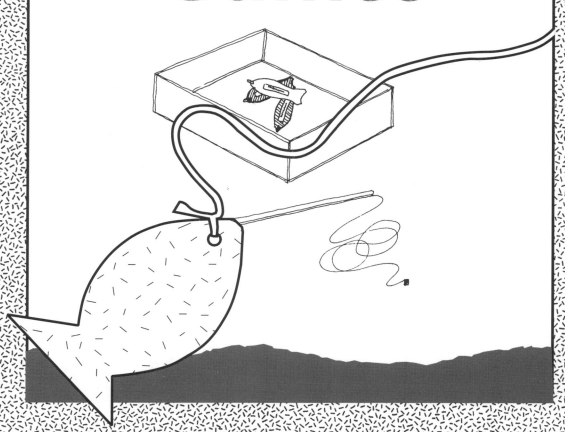

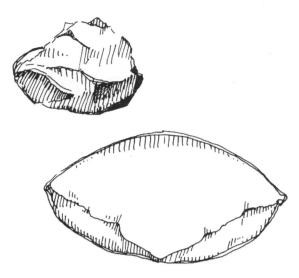

es

...es for the chil-
...e following:

...at is _____.

_____.

___.

a green light means

...w is _____.

A sh... appy, but tears show
you're _____
A table top is flat, but a ball is _____.
Candy is sweet, but a lemon is _____.
A baby is short, but a man is _____.
Glass is smooth, but sandpaper is _____.
Nighttime is dark, but daytime is _____.
A yell is loud, but a whisper is _____.

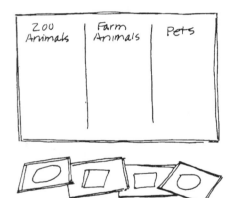

What Kind of Animal?

Divide a poster into three categories, using a ruler and a felt-tip marker. Label the three sections: *Zoo Animals, Farm Animals,* and *Pets.* Gather many pictures of these three kinds of animals for the preschoolers to categorize. Mount the pictures on construction paper.

Place the animal pictures beside the poster. Encourage the preschoolers to place each picture under the proper category.

Sequencing Pictures

Provide pictures showing various stages of Jesus' life—His birth, the visit of the Wise Men, the trip to the Temple at 12, and helping people as a man. Guide the children to arrange the pictures in the correct order.

Variations: Sequencing pictures may be done with pictures of (1) a plant growing, (2) an animal, or (3) with people.

Daytime/Nighttime

Cut out and mount on construction paper pictures of people involved in activities—pictures representing things done at nighttime and other pictures of daytime activities. Place a picture under each child's chair or give a picture to each child.

Provide two large envelopes, one with *Day* printed on it and the other with *Night* on it. Ask each child to tell what the person in his picture is doing. Then he is to place his picture in the appropriate envelope.

Some of the activities may take place during both daytime and nighttime; therefore, they may be correctly placed in either envelope.

A Feeling Game

Provide a paper bag, a shallow box, and two each of objects such as buttons, keys, crayons, books, spoons, rocks, etc.

Place one object of each pair in the box. Put the other object of each pair into the sack. A child chooses an object out of the box. Then he feels into the sack to find the object that matches. He places the pair of objects together, then attempts to match another pair.

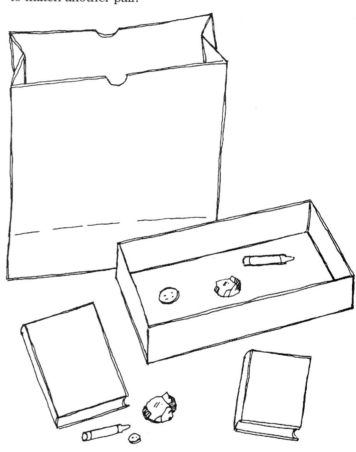

Exploring with Magnets

Provide several kinds of magnets, such as bar magnets, a round magnet, and a horseshoe magnet. Provide one box, similar to a hosiery box, and objects that will be attracted by the magnets, as well as objects that will not. Open the box for the child to use both the top and the bottom. Ask her to place the objects the magnets pick up in one box and the objects the magnets will not pick up in the other box.

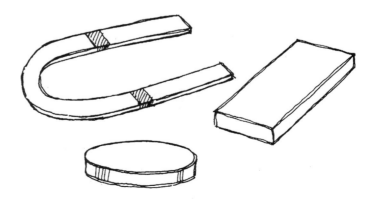

Name the Helper

Place on the floor, in a large sack, some items used by workers in different occupations. Some of the items could be: a newspaper, an empty milk carton, a letter, a stethoscope, a hammer, a whistle, a thermometer, and a can of food.

Ask a child to close his eyes and pull out one of the items from the sack. Ask him which worker might use this article. If the child doesn't know the answer, he may choose a friend to help him. After responding, he chooses someone to have the next turn.

Mystery Pictures

Choose five or six teaching pictures of Bible characters familiar to the preschoolers. Cut a piece of manila paper the size of each picture. Then cut "windows" at strategic places , leaving the windows attached (cut only three sides). Number the windows on the outside to be visible when the window are closed.

The child opens the first window he selects and tries to guess the Bible character or characters in the picture. He continues to open additional windows until he guesses correctly. Then another child has a turn.

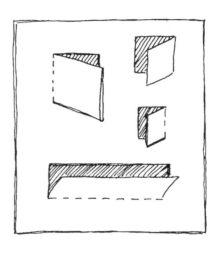

Choose the Lid

Gather a variety of sizes of plastic jars. Remove the lids. Place all the jars and lids in a box. Encourage preschoolers to find the correct lid for each jar.

This game develops visual discrimination, as well as coordination in screwing on the lids.

Good Foods

For a brief game, ask a child to think of a food that helps our bodies grow strong. The child gives the group a hint about the food item (color, size, texture). The preschoolers may take turns describing other food items for the group to guess.

Complete a Bible Verse

Divide a poster into three, four, or five sections, according to the ages of the preschoolers. Print a simple Bible verse in each section of the poster board.

Ask a child to gently toss a beanbag onto one section of the poster. Read part of the verse printed on the section on which the beanbag lands. Ask the child to supply the missing word(s) to the verse.

Variations: This may be used with any unit as a review game. Print a question in each section instead of a Bible verse.

A Sorting Game

Make a three-part frame by taping together three 8-by-11 inch cardboard pieces. Find pictures of an animal, a person, and a food to mount on construction paper. Then glue one picture to each part of the frame.

Collect additional magazine pictures of animals, people, and foods, mount them on construction paper, and cover with clear self-adhesive plastic for durability.

Place these pictures in a box. Instruct a child that she is to take a picture from the box, then decide whether it is an animal, person, or food. She places that picture in front of the frame that it matches. Continue this process until all of the pictures are categorized into three stacks.

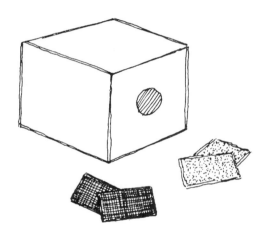

Touch and Tell

Find a box about 12 inches square with all sides closed. Cut a hole (large enough for a child's hand) on two opposite sides of the box. Inside of the box place two pieces each of sandpaper, net material, velvet, lace, satin, and broadcloth.

Lead a child to reach in with both hands and try to find the two pieces that match. He then pulls them out to see if he has guessed correctly. He chooses someone to have the next turn.

A Happy-Sad Game

Provide two sacks: one with a happy face drawn on a paper plate and glued to it, the other with a sad face drawn on a paper plate and glued to it. Print under each respective face, *happy* or *sad*.

From outdated literature and magazines, cut pictures depicting happy and sad people. Mount these pictures to make them colorful. Place pictures in a box.

The preschoolers take turns placing the pictures either in the happy or sad sack according to whether they interpret the people as being happy or sad.

Fishing

Cut fish shapes from construction paper and place a paper clip on each fish. Also, print a Bible thought/verse on each fish. Provide about a 17-inch long stick for a pole, tying a piece of string to the end of the pole with a magnet on the end of the string.

· Place the fish cutouts in a medium-sized box. Let the preschoolers take turns fishing by dropping the magnet onto a paper clip on a fish. After the fish is caught, whisper the Bible thought to the child for him to share with the group. Another way is to read a portion of the thought and let the child complete it.

Variation: Instead of using Bible thoughts, write a question about a story or the unit of study on each fish as a review.

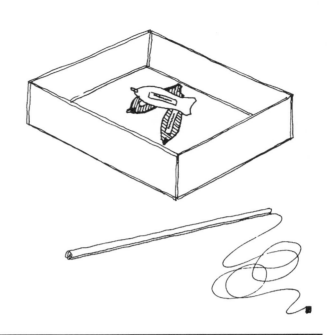

Counting Cotton Balls

Place cotton balls in a sack. Suggest that a preschooler reach into the sack and grab a handful of cotton balls. Help him count how many cotton balls he has. Allow other preschoolers to have a turn.

Variations: (1) Make a set of counting cards, from 1-5 or 1-10, according to the ages of the children. Draw one circle on the first card, two circles on the second card, etc. Ask the preschoolers to place one cotton ball on top of each circle on the cards. Older preschoolers may not need anything except the numerals on the cards. (2) Give a five-year-old child 10 to 20 cotton balls. Ask her to line up the cotton balls on a table in rows of two. Count the cotton balls by twos.

Circle of Colors

For twos and threes, make a cardboard circle of colors to match the colors of plastic clothespins you purchase in a package.

Give a clothespin to each child. Hold the colored cardboard circle for everyone to see. Ask each child to take a turn to attach the clothespin to the matching color on the circle.

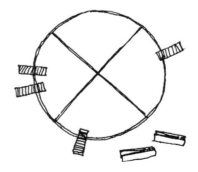

Simple Dramatizations

Plan with the children a simple way to act out a story. Choose actors for the story, and on another day repeat the drama using other actors. At first it is wise for the adult to relate the story as the boys and girls put action to it. Sometimes the adult may call on an actor to say a sentence or two, as appropriate.

Distinguishing Colors

Cut small fish shapes out of three colors of construction paper. Place the shapes in a shoe box with a large hole cut in the lid.

Cover three empty cans with construction paper to match each of the colors of the fish. Lead the preschoolers to pretend they are fishing through an ice hole. They reach through the hole to "catch" a fish. They sort the fish by placing them in the appropriate cans.

(For five-year-olds, use five colors of fish shapes and five colored cans to make the game more difficult.)

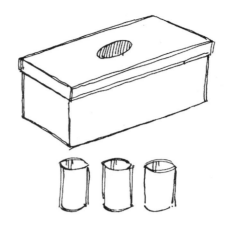

Matching Shapes

Cut circle, square, triangle, and rectangle shapes from different colors of construction paper.

Give each child three shapes. Keep one set of shapes or more for the leader. Hold up a shape and say:

One, two, three
What do you see?
Is yours like this?
Bring it to me.

The child who has the same shape and color brings it to the leader. Repeat the game until all have had a turn or until the children lose interest.

Picture Cube

Make a cardboard cube or purchase a plastic cube. Tape a picture to each side of the cube.

A child tosses or rolls the cube. When the cube stops rolling, the child describes the picture on top of the cube. The adult asks questions to stimulate conversation.

Continue by selecting another child to toss the cube.

Variation: Place a different color on each side of the cube for a child to toss and then identify the color on the top of the cube.

Concentration

Make a matching game using index cards or small plastic lids from potato-chip cans. Purchase stickers (preferably with fairly large pictures) from a greeting card shop, or cut identical pictures from magazines. Stick one sticker to each card, making six matching sets for five-year-olds, five matching sets for fours, and perhaps only three matching sets for threes. (Much will depend on the development of the preschoolers.)

To play, turn the cards over where the pictures will not be seen. The first child turns up two cards trying to make a match. He must show the pictures to all of those playing, naming the objects on the cards. If they match, he holds them. If not, they are placed in the same spots where they were for another person to have a turn.

Concentration games may be made by collecting pictures (two alike) or stickers of insects, animals, flowers, birds, colors, numbers, furniture, people, and other things.

Listening Ears

Provide a paper bag with the following articles inside: a baby rattle, a bell, keys on a key ring, a baby's squeaky toy, and a crumpled piece of paper. The adult reaches into the bag, and makes a sound with an item. The preschoolers try to guess what it is.

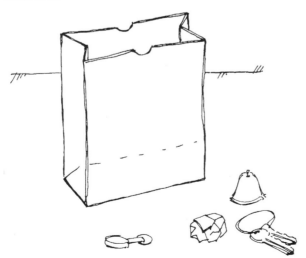

Guess the Number

Place several fall leaves in a see-through jar or container. Ask the preschoolers to guess how many leaves are inside. Remove the leaves from the jar and count them together. How many guessed too high? How many guessed too low?

Who Am I?

Use descriptions of various occupations for others to guess. Adapt some of the following:

I wear a badge. Sometimes I drive a car and sometimes I ride a motorcycle. Who am I? (police officer)

I wear a white uniform and white shoes. I help the doctor. Who am I? (nurse)

I deliver letters, postcards, and packages to your home. Who am I? (mail carrier)

I work with all kinds of flowers and plants. I make corsages and flower arrangements. Who am I? (florist)

I wear a bright red hat and drive a red truck. Who am I? (fire fighter)

I drive a white truck that is filled with something that is good for you to drink. I sometimes work when you are sleeping. Who am I? (milk carrier)

I work on pipes. If you have a leak in your kitchen sink or in your bathroom, your parents call me to repair it. Who am I? (plumber)

I work on something that looks like a type-writer. I look at a screen to see what I've written rather than looking at a piece of paper. Who am I? (computer operator)

Sometimes your parents call me to come to your house to stay with you when they are going to be away. Who am I? (baby-sitter)

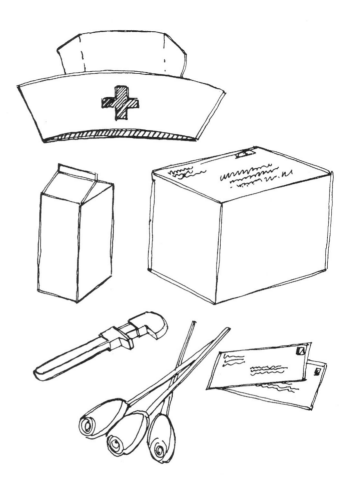

Nesting Toys

Assemble several plastic cups or small boxes of various sizes so that they will fit one inside the other. This is a good problem-solving activity for young preschoolers because it involves dexterity and discrimination skills.

Identifying Sounds

Ask the preschooler to close their eyes, place their hands over them, and listen carefully with their ears. Provide some of the following sounds for the children to identify: humming, triangle, bell, Autoharp, snapping fingers, tone blocks, clapping hands, and shuffling feet.

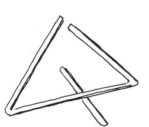

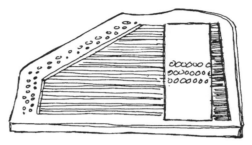

What Does the Seed Grow?

Make a seed-matching game to be played individually or with a group. Glue one or two seeds that are alike from five fruits on 3-by-5-inch cards. On five other cards, glue a picture of each fruit.

Cover the cards with clear self-adhesive plastic.

Ask a child to examine the seeds and pictures and try to pair them according to the ones that go together.

What Do You Hear?

Walk outside. Ask the children to close their eyes and listen carefully. Tell them to open their eyes and tell what sounds they heard.

Time Is Important

Provide a kitchen timer or stop watch. Help the preschoolers keep a record of the length of time it takes them to do various activities such as read a book, work a puzzle, paint a picture, etc. Do this activity on rare occasions to offer variety.

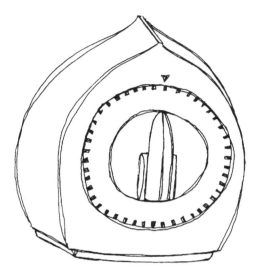

Picture Posing

Choose a picture with several characters. Talk about the picture. Select a child to represent each person in the picture. Ask the children to look at the picture and to place themselves in positions like the people in the picture.

Matching Pairs

Collect some things that you can find two alike. Place these articles in a box, mixing them up. Encourage the children to match the objects. Try to find two of the following:

several pairs of socks   spools of thread
jar rings   keys
pencils   rubber bands
pair of gloves or   birthday candles
mittens   napkin rings
plastic spoons

Drama Using Puppets

Lead the preschoolers to cut out figures of persons and objects from catalogs or magazines. Mount these on cardboard. Then guide each child to punch a small hole in her cutout and run a string through it. Make the string long enough to reach from the child's waist almost to the floor. One end is tied to the puppet and the other end may have a small loop so that a finger can easily slip through it.

Encourage the boys and girls to use the string puppets to act out a favorite story. To simplify this activity, the adult may tell the story as the puppets act it out.

Matching Indian Symbols

Cut cardboard into 12 four-inch squares. Color or paint one Indian symbol on two squares to make six matching sets. These symbols may be used in different ways: as a concentration game, as a group matching game (the adult holds up one square for a child to choose the symbol that matches), or as an individual quiet activity (one child works alone to find the two that are alike to complete each set).

Leaf Pairs

Gather six pairs of fall leaves. Press the leaves between heavy books for several days. Mount each leaf on a heavy piece of cardboard, print the name of the tree on the cardboard, and cover the entire piece with clear self-adhesive plastic. Ask the children to match the pairs of leaves. Help the five-year-olds to know the kind of tree from which the leaf came.

See What You Can Find

Go for a nature walk. Place a masking tape bracelet on each child. (Bracelets are made by securing masking tape strips, sticky side out, around each child's wrist.) Ask each child to stick some things to his "bracelet" to take back to the room. Also point out some things in nature which cannot be taken back: clouds, trees, sun, etc.

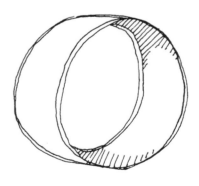

Guess the Animal Friend

Ask the boys and girls to close their eyes. Select one child to tiptoe to the back of the room and imitate an animal sound. With their eyes closed, the children are to try to name the person making the animal sound.

Suggest that the child choose a friend to repeat this action while the children's eyes are closed.

What Does the Cow Give Us?

Make a set of pictures matching farm animals with what they give us. Examples: cow-milk; chicken-eggs; pig-bacon, etc. Guide the preschoolers to match the animals with the item they provide for us.

Summer or Winter

On one piece of construction paper, glue a summertime picture and print *Summer* underneath the picture. On another color of construction paper, glue a wintertime picture and print *Winter* underneath the picture. Gather a number of pictures depicting these two seasons for the boys and girls to sort.

For five-year-olds, include all four seasons in the game.

How Much Does It Weigh?

Provide some kitchen scales for the children to weigh many different things. It is difficult for young ones to realize that something small but heavy can weigh more than something that is large but lightweight.

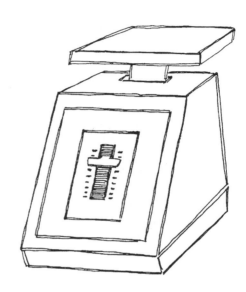

Guess the Story

Lead the children to illustrate a favorite story using crayons or felt-tip markers. When all the pictures are finished, let the others guess each story illustrated.

Variations: Ask the children to illustrate one of the animals in Noah's ark. Then the children try to guess what each animal is.

Mothers and Their Babies

Find pictures of mother animals and their babies to make a matching set. Try to find some of the following:

cow-calf	eagle-eaglet
dog-puppy	owl-owlet
cat-kitten	goose-gosling
horse-colt	duck-duckling
chicken-chick	sheep-lamb

What Do You Smell?

Use five or six unbreakable containers (film containers or something similar) to make a set of items to smell and identify. Place a cotton ball in each container. Sprinkle one of the following on top of each piece of cotton: onion salt, cinnamon, coffee, cocoa, talcum powder, and dry mustard.

Ask a child to cover his eyes, sniff one of the cans, and guess what the odor is.

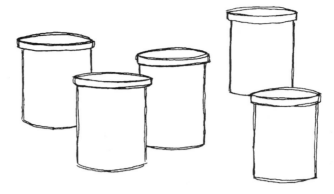

Whose Shadow?

Hang a sheet, and place a light behind it. Ask children to cover their eyes and put their heads in their laps (no peeking). The adult taps one child to go behind the sheet. Other children open their eyes to guess whose shadow they see.

Cleaning the Room

Tune, "London Bridge"

We will all help clean the room,
   Clean the room, clean the room.
We will all help clean the room,
   We are helpers.

It is a special learning experience for preschoolers to know how to put away toys and clean a room.

Chapter 3

Musical *Games*

The peo-ple on the bus go up and down, up and down, up and down. The peo-ple on the bus go up and down, around the town.

Who Has Joined Our Group?

As the preschoolers come together for an activity or for group time, sing to the tune of "The Farmer in the Dell":

One has joined our group.
Two have joined our group.
Heigh-o, the derry-o,
Four have joined our group.

Adjust the italicized number to the actual number who has come to group time. Continue singing and counting until most of the children are in the group.

Getting Exercise

This activity may be done with the very young child, if you hold his hands and follow the words of the song. Middle and older preschoolers will prefer doing the actions their own way.
Tune, "The Farmer in the Dell":

We're walking in the room,
We're walking in the room,
Oh, we need the exercise,
We're walking in the room.

Add other verses, but keep line three the same. Other suggestions: jumping up and down, twisting side to side, hopping in the room, stretching way up high, running in our place.

Beat the Rhythm

Use a drum (homemade or purchased) to beat rhythm patterns that suggest various ways for preschoolers to move around the room. The rhythms may include walking, marching, running, skipping, tiptoeing, galloping, and stomping.

Variation: The adult plays one tapping pattern on the drum for a child to imitate that pattern. Allow other children to take turns imitating the pattern the adult originates. The patterns may be: tap-tap-stop, tap-tap-stop; tap-tap-tap, tap-tap-tap; tap-tap-tap-tap, tap-tap-tap-tap; tap-stop-tap-stop, tap-stop-tap-stop.

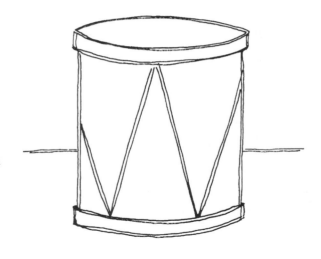

Skating in Socks

Suggest the preschoolers skate in the room as you sing to the tune of "Row, Row, Row Your Boat":

Slide, slide, slide your feet,
All across the floor.
Skating, skating, skating, skating,
Let's do it some more.

Variation: Preschoolers use their hands to pretend to be skating.

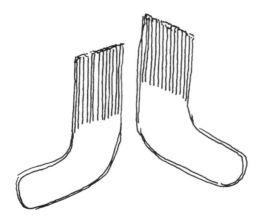

Using Crepe Paper Streamers

Cut a strip of crepe paper about 30 inches long for each child. Give each child a streamer to use for rhythms. Choose a recording (preferably with instrumental music only). Suggest that the preschoolers move around, using their streamers to make large and small circles, sometimes close to the floor, sometimes high, sometimes to the side, or any way they choose.

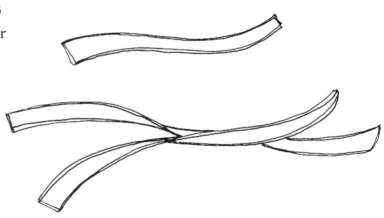

Variation: Scarves or ribbons may be used instead of the crepe paper streamers.

Who Has Red on?

Boys and girls enjoy this song because each child receives recognition. As a color is mentioned in the song, the child examines her clothing from head to foot. If she is wearing that color, she stands. The entire group sings the first part asking the question. The group standing responds with the second part.

Who has red on? Who has red on? Who is wearing red? Who is wearing red?

The group standing responds:

We are wearing red, We are wearing red. We wear red; we wear red.

Sing many verses substituting a different color each time to be certain that all children have at least one opportunity to stand.

Sing as You Go

This song can be adapted to any excursion. Tune, "She'll Be Coming 'Round the Mountain":
  We are going on a trip to the zoo.
  We are going on a trip to the zoo.
  We're excited as can be,
  'Cause there's much we want to see,
  Yes, we're going on a trip to the zoo.

31

Will You Be a Friend of Mine?

The group join hands to make a circle. Then, drop hands. Choose one child to be "It." That child walks around the circle as you sing the question. "It" stands in front of a friend on the last line of the first verse. As the group sings the second part of the song, the two walk around the circle together.

As you go back to the question, these two children line up behind each other because each one will choose a friend this time. Therefore, there will be two couples walking as you sing the second part of the song. Continue until everyone is a partner. Tune, "Merrily We Roll Along":

Will you be a friend of mine,
Friend of mine, friend of mine?
Will you be a friend of mine,
And walk around with me?

I will be a friend of yours,
Friend of yours, friend of yours.
I will be a friend of yours,
And walk around with you.

Name That Tune

If you have a piano, play some tunes that are familiar to the preschoolers for them to guess. If there is no instrument, hum some of the children's favorite songs as that will work just as well.

After a child guesses each song, suggest that the group sing it.

I Have a Good Friend

Using a beanbag, toss it to a child as you sing or chant:

I have a good friend
Larry is his name.

Larry then tosses the beanbag to another child as the group chants or sings these words. Continue until all of the preschoolers have been called by name.

Wiggle Game

Ask the preschoolers to place both feet together. If the floor has tile squares, they may place both feet in one block. Suggest that the children try to wiggle many parts of their bodies without moving their feet. Play a brief recording to which they keep time as they move in a variety of ways.

Surprise Box

Find a durable cardboard box, small enough for the children to handle, but large enough to hold some article used in the room. Cover the box with wrapping paper or colorful self-adhesive plastic to make it attractive.

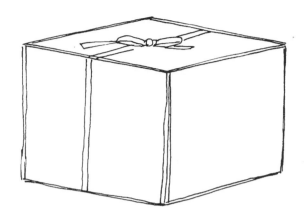

Place a surprise in the box, tie the lid, and let the boys and girls pass the box around the group. Play a recording (or piano) while the box is passed.

The child holding the box when the music stops gets to open it and display the surprise. The surprise may be a ball, a game to play, a new book to read, pictures to look at and talk about, a recording to play, a nature item, or something new for the room.

A Clapping Game

For a brief game, clap the rhythm of several familiar songs. The preschoolers guess the song the adult is clapping. After guessing the name, the group sings it together.

Listen and Wiggle

Ask the children to wiggle their bodies as you ring a bell and to stand very still when the bell is quiet.

Come on and Join into the Game

Folk Song

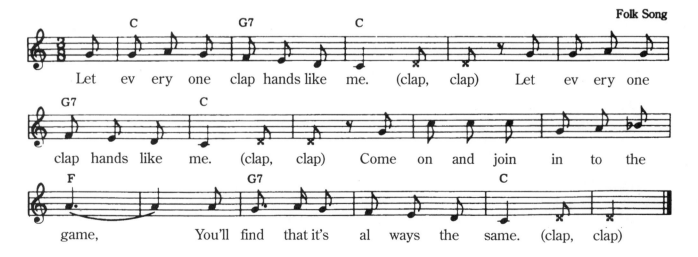

Let ev ery one clap hands like me. (clap, clap) Let ev ery one clap hands like me. (clap, clap) Come on and join in to the game, You'll find that it's al ways the same. (clap, clap)

Other verses may include: stamp feet, turn around, reach high (reach high and snap fingers), blink eyes, yawn, laugh, cry, sleep.

Animal Fun

Tune: "Here We Go 'Round the Mulberry Bush"

This is the way the rabbit hops,
Rabbit hops, rabbit hops.
This is the way the rabbit hops
Out in the forest.

This is the way the kangaroo jumps,
Kangaroo jumps, kangaroo jumps.
This is the way the kangaroo jumps
Out in the desert.

This is the way the elephant walks,
Elephant walks, elephant walks.
This is the way the elephant walks
Out in the jungle.

This is the way the fish swim,
The fish swim, the fish swim.
This is the way the fish swim,
Down in the river.

This is the way the chicken walks,
The chicken walks, the chicken walks,
This is the way the chicken walks,
Down on the farm.

This is the way the little lamb runs,
The little lamb runs, the little lamb runs.
This is the way the little lamb runs,
Out on the hillside.

Row, Row, Row Your Boat

Each child needs a partner. In case the number is uneven, and adult may be a partner with one of the preschoolers.

The partners sit on the floor facing each other with legs straight out in front. If possible, they should place the soles of their shoes together. Then they grasp hands and hold on tightly.

As one person leans back, the other leans forward and vice versa. Sing "Row, Row, Row Your Boat" as you "row" in time to the music, back and forth. Repeat this several times for fun.

Our Family

Tune, "Down by the Station"
  See our little fam'ly,
  Early in the morning.
  All getting dressed
  To go to our "work."
  First, we have breakfast,
  Then we brush our teeth,
  Good-bye, good-bye,
  Away we go.

Lead the preschoolers to pantomime the actions in the song.

Choosing Songs

Choose a plastic detergent bottle and wash it thoroughly. Cut off the top in order to insert some slips of paper. Cut five or more pieces of construction paper on which the title of a favorite song is written.

Place the bottle in the center of the group, and choose one child to spin it. The one to whom the bottle points gets to pull out a strip of paper. The adult reads the name of the song, and preschoolers sing it. Continue until each song has been sung.

I Wish I Were a . . .

Tune: "Did You Ever See a Lassie?"

I wish I were a farmer, a farmer, a farmer,
I wish I were a farmer, I know what I'd do.
I'd dig holes and plant seeds; I'd dig holes and
    plant seeds.
I wish I were a farmer, I know what I'd do.

When preschoolers sing the third and fourth
    lines, they may pretend to dig with a hoe.

I wish I were a doctor, a doctor, a doctor,
I wish I were a doctor, I know what I'd do.
I'd write a prescription to help folks get well.
I wish I were a doctor, I know what I'd do.

Children may pretend to be writing as they sing
    the third and fourth lines.

I wish I were a preacher, a preacher, a preacher.
I wish I were a preacher, I know what I'd do.
I'd read from my Bible, I'd read from my Bible.
I wish I were a preacher, I know what I'd do.

Preschooler may cup hands to make a Bible as
    they sing the third and fourth lines.

I wish I were a missionary, a missionary, a
    missionary.
I wish I were a missionary, I know what I'd do.
I'd tell about Jesus, I'd tell about Jesus.
I wish I were a missionary, I know what I'd do.

Each preschooler may turn to the one next to
him as though talking about Jesus as they sing the
third and fourth lines.

What Do You Do?

Tune, "The Muffin Man"

Oh, what do you do when the light turns green, The light turns green, the light turns green?
You cross the street when the light turns green, The light turns green, the light turns green.

Oh, what do you do when the light turns green On the way to *school*? (*church*)
You cross the street when the light turns green On the way to *school*? (*church*)

Words by Mary Jaye; arranged by Darrell Peter
From *Making Music Your Own—K*, © 1971 Silver Burdett Company. All rights reserved. Used by permission.

3. Oh, what do you do when the light turns red?
4. You stop and wait when the light turns red . . .

5. Oh, what do you do when the light turns yellow . . .
6. You do not cross when the light turns yellow . . .

Thanksgiving Day Is Coming

Tune, "The Bear Went Over the Mountain"

Thanksgiving Day is coming;
Thanksgiving Day is coming;
Thanksgiving Day is coming
And we're so glad.

(Group forms circle. Slide to the right on the first line; slide to the left on second line; slide to the right on the third line; stand still and clap hands)

We'll have some turkey and dressing;
We'll have some turkey and dressing;
We'll have some turkey and dressing;
And we're so glad.

(Repeat actions as given for first stanza.)

Variations: This singing game may be adapted to other holidays:

(1) Christmas—Second stanza: We'll celebrate Jesus' birthday.

(2) Valentine's Day—Second stanza: We'll have some big, red hearts.

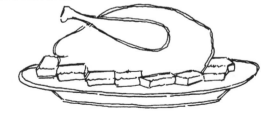

36

If You Lived Far Away

Tune, "The Farmer in the Dell"
> Oh, if you lived in Spain,
> Oh, if you lived in Spain,
> If you lived in Spain,
> Oh, what would you do?

Children walk around the circle as they sing. A child may answer what he would do if he lived in Spain. This song may be adapted to any place being studied.

Indian Dance

Choose a recording with some music typical of Indians, or use a drum to give an Indian beat. Talk about how Indians dance—basically bearing weight on first the toes of one foot, and then the heel of the same foot. Alternate feet using: toe, heel, toe, heel, etc.

Variations: run to the drum beat, walk to the drum beat, hop to the drum beat, jump to the drum beat, hop on one foot, etc.

Musical Balls

Cut out enough construction paper or lightweight cardboard balls (about 12 inches in diameter) for the number of children playing, less one. Place one ball on the floor for each child. Play a short part of a recording or something on the piano for the children to move around to the music. When the music stops, each child is to stand on a ball.

One child will be without a ball each time but just laugh and play the game again. Remember that competition is inappropriate for preschoolers because every child wants to be a winner. Losing is difficult for them. Help each to safely land on a ball sometimes.

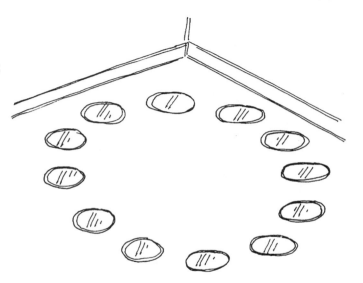

Snowflakes Falling

Provide white crepe-paper streamers or white scarves for the children to pretend to be snowflakes. Choose a recording with a fast tempo to act out snowflakes on a windy day. Play a recording with fairly slow tempo for them to be snowflakes softly falling.

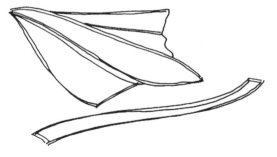

Galloping Horses

Provide several wooden horses for the preschoolers to pretend to be galloping horses. Some children will enjoy galloping without a "horse."

The Bus Song

Adapted

The peo-ple on the bus go up and down,
up and down, up and down. The peo-ple on the
bus go up and down, all around the town.

Additional verses:

The horn on the bus goes beep, beep, beep. (Press horn with fist.)

The wipers on the bus go swish, swish, swish. (Hold arms out and imitate wipers by waving them right and left.)

The money on the bus goes clink, clink, clink. (Snap fingers along with the *clink*.)

The baby on the bus goes, "wah, wah, wah." (Fold arms and pretend to rock baby.)

The driver on the bus says, "Please, move back." (Fold fingers and use thumb to point to the back.)

The bell on the bus goes ding, ding, ding. (Raise hand up and down as though pulling a cord to ring the bell.)

Make Your Own Music

Use a set of eight glasses with varying amounts of water. When the glasses are tapped with a rhythm stick, they will make various tones. Let the children experiment with the pouring to try to get a one-octave range of notes. Five-year-olds may play some simple tunes like "Mary Had a Little Lamb."

Here Comes the Train

Discuss with the preschoolers about various ways the children may become a train, each representing one car. They could put their hands on the shoulder of the person in front of them, or they could put their hands on the hips of the person in front. Let the children sing a song about the train or play a recording or the piano as they pretend to be a train.

The Farmer Plants His Seed

Tune, "The Farmer in the Dell" (Use appropriate actions)

The farmer plants his seed;
The farmer plants his seed.
Hi-ho, the derry-o,
The farmer plants his seed.

Verse 2: The rain begins to fall.
Verse 3: The sun begins to shine.
Verse 4: The wind begins to blow.
Verse 5: The food begins to grow.

'Round and 'Round the Village

Folk Song

Go 'round and 'round the vil-lage. Go 'round and 'round the vil-lage. Go

'round and 'round the vil lage. Let's have some fun to - day.

(Children join hands to form a circle. They walk around the circle singing the first verse.)

Let's fly around the village.
(Pretend to be airplanes)
Let's skip around the village.

Let's drive around the village.
(Pretend to be cars)
Let's gallop around the village.
(Pretend to ride horses)

A Rainy Day Song

Tune, "If You're Happy and You Know It"

I like to hear the rain as it comes down. (tap, tap)
I like to hear the rain as it comes down. (tap, tap)
It softly hits the ground
And puddles all around.
Oh, I like to hear the rain as it comes down.
   (splash, splash)

Reading

Tune, "Mary Had a Little Lamb"
How we like to read good books,
Read good books, read good books.
How we like to read good books,
At our school (church).

We read of places we can't go,
We can't go, we can't go.
We read of places we can't go
Except through imagination.

Looby Loo

English Game Song

Refrain:

Here we go Loo - by Loo, Here we go Loo - by light,

Here we go Loo - by Loo, All on a Sat - ur - day night.

Stanza:

1. I put my right hand in, I take my right hand out,
2. I put my left hand in, I take my left hand out,

I give my right hand a shake, shake, shake And turn my-self a bout.
I give my left hand a shake, shake, shake And turn my-self a bout.

Actions:

The children form a circle holding hands. Each time they sing the chorus, they move three steps inside the circle and three steps out (backwards). With the stanzas, they drop hands, face the center of the circle, and act out the words.

3. I put my right foot in, etc.
4. I put my left foot in, etc.
5. I put my head in, etc.
6. I put my whole self in, etc.

(For groups younger than five, do not stress right and left. Just accept either.)

We Are Happy

Tune, "Are You Sleeping?"
    We are happy;
    We are happy.
    We have fun;
    We have fun.
    Playing with the blocks;
    Playing with the blocks.
    Build a church;
    Build a church.

(Adapt the last two lines: house, castle, tower, bridge.)

Variation: Instead of *playing with the blocks,* adapt to another area, such as *playing in our house; rock the baby.*

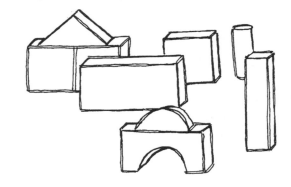

Bend and Touch Your Toes

Tune, "London Bridge Is Falling Down"

Can you bend and touch your toes,
Touch your toes, touch your toes?
Can you bend and touch your toes;
Then turn around?

Can you reach up very high,
Very high, very high?
Can you reach up very high;
Then be seated?

Six Little Ducks

Folk Song

Six lit-tle ducks that I once knew, Fat ones, skin-ny ones, fair ones, too.

Chorus:

But the one lit-tle duck with a feath-er on his back,

He led the oth-ers with his quack, quack, quack.

Quack, quack quack, quack, quack, quack

He led the oth-ers with his quack, quack, quack.

Down to the river they would go,
Wibble, wobble, wibble, wobble, to and fro.

Repeat chorus

Elephant Song

Chilean Folk Song

One el-e-phant went out to play, Out on a spi-der's web one day.

He had such e - nor- mous fun, He called for a-noth-er el - e -phant to come.

Two el-e-phants went out to play,
Out on a spider's web one day.
They had such enormous fun,
They called for a-noth-er el-e-phant to come.

Choose one child to be the elephant. For the second verse, that child chooses the second ele-phant. Repeat until *They called for another but*

there was none. If time is limited, sing *He called for all the elephants to come.*

To pretend to be elephants, the preschoolers bend over with hands clasped in front to make a trunk. Each "elephant" sways his trunk and walks in time to the music.

Hey, Betty Martin!

Folk Song

Hey, Bet - ty Mar - tin,* tip - py toe, tip - py toe,

Hey, Bet -ty Mar - tin, tip - toe do, Hey, Bet - ty Mar - tin,

tip - py toe, tip - py toe, Hey, Bet -ty Mar - tin, We like you.

*Use a child's name.
Actions: skip around, jump around, march around,
hop around, crawl around.

Noble Duke of York

English Game Song

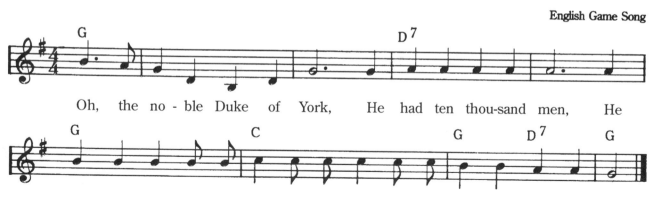

Oh, the no-ble Duke of York, He had ten thou-sand men, He

marched them up to the top of the hill, And he marched them down a - gain.

Now when they were up, they were up,
And when they were down, they were down;
But when they were only halfway up,
They were neither up nor down.

Hold up ten fingers and wiggle them.
Use hands in ascending, climbing motion.
Use hands in descending motion.
Hold arms overhead on up
Drop arms toward floor on down.
Hold arms straight ahead.
Overhead on up *and down toward floor on* down.

Skip to My Lou

Folk Song

Fly in the but - ter - milk, shoo, fly, shoo! Fly in the but -ter - milk, shoo, fly, shoo!

Fly in the but - ter - milk, shoo, fly, shoo! Skip to my lou, my dar - ling.

Actions: walk, tiptoe, jump.
Children join hands in a circle and go around with
the indicated action.

Have You Ever Seen a Lassie?

Folk Song

Players join hands to form a circle. "It" is placed in the center. The group sings, adapting the word *lassie* to *laddie* when a boy is "It."
As the group sings *this way and that way,* the one in the center does some action for the others to imitate. For example: she may hop around, jump up and down, reach for the sky, and touch toes, etc.

Playing Instruments

F   C⁷   Folk Song

This is the way we tap our sticks, tap our sticks, tap our sticks.

This is the way we tap our sticks, When we want to make mu - sic.

This is the way we ring our bells,
ring our bells, ring our bells.
This is the way we ring our bells,
When we want to make mu - sic.

This is the way we beat the drum,
beat the drum, beat the drum.
This is the way we beat the drum,
When we want to make mu - sic.

Several preschoolers play instruments as everyone
sings. The children without instruments pantomime playing them.

Pop! Goes the Weasel

American Folk Song

1. A pen - ny for a spool of thread, A pen - ny for a nee - dle,
2. — All a - round the chick - en coop The mon - key chased the wea - sel,

That's the way the mon - ey goes, Pop! goes the wea - sel.

Preschoolers clap as they sing the word *pop*.

Five Little Chickadees

Singing Game

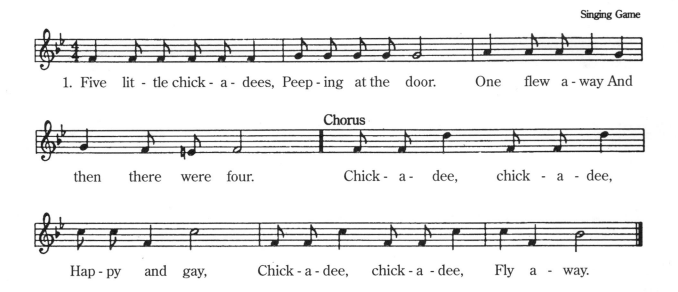

1. Five lit - tle chick - a - dees, Peep - ing at the door. One flew a - way And then there were four.

Chorus

Chick - a - dee, chick - a - dee, Hap - py and gay, Chick - a - dee, chick - a - dee, Fly a - way.

2. Four lit - tle chick-a-dees, Sit - ting in a tree.
One flew away And then there were three.

3. Three lit - tle chick-a-dees, Look - ing at you.
One flew a - way And then there were two.

4. Two lit - tle chick - a - dees, Sit - ting in the sun, One flew a - way And then there was one.

5. One lit - tle chick - a - dee, Left all a - lone, It flew away And then there was none.

Five preschoolers sit on the floor in a row. A chickadee gets up, flies about, and leaves the others as each stanza is sung.

Chapter 4

Poems and *Fingerplays*

Jack-in-the-Box

Jack-in-the-box, all shut up tight
   (make a fist with thumb tucked inside),
Not a breath of air, not a ray of light.
How dark it must be!
He cannot see.
But open the lid
And up jumps he. (pull thumb up quickly)

Author unknown

Where Is Thumb Man?

(May be sung to the tune of "Are You Sleeping?")
   Where is thumb man? (hands behind back)
   Where is thumb man?
   Here I am. (one fist forward with thumb
     standing)
   Here I am. (other fist forward, thumb standing)
   How do you do this morning? (wiggle one
     thumb in direction of other)
   Very well, I thank you. (wiggle other thumb)
   Run away, run away. (hands behind back again)

Additional verses include fingers:
Where is pointer?
Where is tall man?
Where is ring man?
Where is small man?

Touch Your Nose

Touch your nose,
Touch your chin;
That's the way this game begins.
Touch your eyes,
Touch your knees;
Now pretend you're going to sneeze.
(finger under nose)

Touch your nose,
Touch your hair,
Touch one ear;
Touch two red lips right here.
Touch your elbows
Where they bend;
That's the way this touch game ends.

From *Rhymes for Fingers and Flannelboards,* by Louise Binder
Scott and J. J. Thompson. Copyright 1989. Printed with permission
from the T.S. Denison Co., Inc., Minneapolis, Minnesota.

Grandmother's Glasses

These are grandmother's glasses. (Make glasses
   over eyes)
This is grandmother's cap. (Peak hands on head)
This is the way she folds her hands. (Fold hands)
And puts them in her lap. (Place in lap)
These are grandfather's glasses. (Make glasses
   over eyes)
This is grandfather's hat. (Hand flat on head)
This is the way he folds his arms (Cross arms on
   chest)
And sits there just like that. (Look straight ahead)

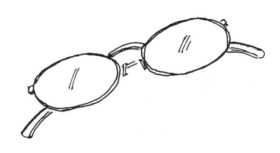

Merry, Old Merry-Go-Round!

(Keep hands on hips except when clapping)

The merry, old merry-go-round (clap, clap!)
Goes up and down and around! (clap, clap!)

(Action: Up on tiptoes, bend knees, and go around
with hips. Repeat this and other actions
throughout.)

It never goes left: (bend left)
It never goes right: (bend right)
Just up and down and around! (clap, clap!)

The merry, old merry-go-round (clap, clap!)
Goes up and down and around! (clap, clap!)
It never goes zig; (twist left)
It never goes zag; (twist right)
It never goes left;
It never goes right:
Just up and down and around (clap, clap!)

The merry, old merry-go-round (clap, clap!)
Goes up and down and around! (clap, clap!)
It never goes in; (bend forward)
It never goes out; (bend backward)
It never goes zig;
It never goes zag;
It never goes left
It never goes right:
Just up and down and around! (clap, clap!)
The merry, old merry-go-round (clap, clap!)
Goes up and down and around! (clap, clap!)
I love it, I do, when I'm riding with you
On the merry, old merry-go-round! (clap, clap!)

"Merry, Old Merry-Go-Round" from LET'S TALK! (Choral speaking format) by Ruth I. Dowell. © 1986. Published and distributed by Pollyanna Productions (P.O. Box 3222, Terre Haute, IN 47803). Ruth is also the author of MOVE OVER, MOTHER GOOSE!

The Rain

Rain on the green grass,
  And rain on the tree,
And rain on the house-top,
  But not upon me!

Author unknown

Little Wind

Little wind, blow on the hilltop,
Little wind, blow on the plain,
Little wind, blow up the sunshine,
Little wind, blow off the rain.

Author unknown

49

This Is Mother

This is mother, (point to the thumb on one hand)
This is father, (point to the pointing finger on same hand)
This is brother tall, (point to tallest finger)
This is sister, (point to ring finger)
This is baby small. (point to little finger)

I Can

I can snap my fingers, I can tap my toes.
I can nod my head, I can wiggle my nose.
I can stretch up high, I can bend down low,
I can sit on the floor and fold my hands just so.

From *Church Weekday Early Education Curriculum Guide for Five-Year-Olds* by Doris Rouse. Copyright 1983 Convention Press. Used by permission.

Five Little Christmas Trees

Preschoolers will hold up one hand with fingers standing tall and straight as they say:

Five little Christmas trees wishing there were more,
One was chopped down and then there were four.

Four little Christmas trees standing for all to see,
One was chopped down and then there were three.

Three little Christmas trees 'neath the sky so blue,
One was chopped down and then there were two.

Two little Christmas trees having lots of fun,
One was chopped down and then there was one.

One little Christmas tree standing all alone,
Out in the woods for that is its home.

Do as I Do

I'll touch my hair, my lips, my eyes;
I'll sit up straight, and then I'll rise;
I'll touch my lips, my nose, my chin,
Then quietly sit down again.

This exercise poem may be varied by touching other body parts. Remember that the third body part must be *eyes* to rhyme with *rise*; the third body part in the third line must be *chin* to rhyme with *again*.

Over in the Meadow

Over in the meadow in the sand in the sun
Lived an old mother turtle and her little turtle
   one.
"Dig," said the mother. "I dig," said the one,
So he dug all day in the sand in the sun.

Over in the meadow where the stream runs blue
Lived an old mother fish and her little fishes two.
"Swim," said the mother. "We swim," said the
   two,
So they swam all day where the stream runs blue.

Over in the meadow in a hole in a tree
Lived an old mother owl and her little owls three.
"Tu-whoo," said the mother. "Tu-whoo," said the
   three,
So they tu-whooed all day in a hole in a tree.

Over in the meadow by the old barn door
Lived an old mother rat and her little ratties four.
"Gnaw," said the mother. "We gnaw," said the
   four,
So they gnawed all day by the old barn door.

Over in the meadow in a snug beehive
Lived an old mother bee and her little bees five.
"Buzz," said the mother. "We buzz," said the five,
So they buzzed all day in a snug beehive.

Over in the meadow in a nest built of sticks
Lived an old mother crow and her little crows six,
"Caw," said the mother. "We caw," said the six,
So they cawed all day in a nest built of sticks.

Over in the meadow where the grass grows even
Lived an old mother frog and her little froggies
   seven.
"Jump," said the mother. "We jump," said the
   seven,
So they jumped all day where the grass grows
   even.

Over in the meadow by the old mossy gate
Lived an old mother lizard and her little lizards
   eight.
"Bask," said the mother. "We bask," said the
   eight,
So they basked all day by the old mossy gate.

Over in the meadow by the old Scotch pine
Lived an old mother duck and her little ducks
   nine,
"Quack," said the mother. "We quack," said the
   nine,
So they quacked all day by the old Scotch pine.

Over in the meadow in a cozy little den
Lived an old mother rabbit and her little rabbits
   ten.
"Hop," said the mother. "We hop," said the ten,
So they hopped all day in a cozy little den.

Old nursery song

Two Mother Pigs

Two mother pigs lived in a pen (hold up thumbs),
Each had four babies, and that made ten (raise all
    fingers on both hands),
These four babies were black as night (extend
    four fingers of one hand),
These four babies were black and white (hold up
    four fingers of other hand).
But all eight babies loved to play
And they rolled and rolled in the mud all day
(wiggle fingers over each other).
At night, with their mothers, they curled up in a
    heap (make a fist),
They closed their eyes and they went to sleep.

Five Little Ducks

Five little ducks went swimming one day,
Over the pond and far away.
Mother duck said, "Quack, quack, quack, quack,"
But only four little ducks came back.

Four little ducks went swimming one day,
Over the pond and far away.
Mother duck said, "Quack, quack, quack, quack,"
But only three little ducks came back.

Three little ducks went swimming one day,
Over the pond and far away.
Mother duck said, "Quack, quack, quack, quack,"
But only two little ducks came back.

Two little ducks went swimming one day,
Over the pond and far away.
Mother duck said, "Quack, quack, quack, quack,"
But only one little duck came back.

One little duck went swimming one day,
Over the pond and far away.
Mother duck said, "Quack, quack, quack, quack,"
But no little ducks came back.

Five little ducks came back one day,
Over the pond and far away.
Mother duck said, "Quack, quack, quack, quack,"
As five little ducks came swimming back.

Hold up fingers to denote the number of ducks.
Make the duck's bill by placing hands together and
opening for the *quack* sound.

From *Eye Winker, Tom Tinker, Chin Chopper—50 Musical Finger-
plays,* by Tom Glazer, Doubleday & Company, New York.

Here's a Ball for Baby

Here's a ball for baby, big and soft and round.
   (Make a ball with two hands)
Here is baby's hammer; see how he can pound.
   (Pound on one fist with another)
Here is baby's music, clapping, clapping, so.
   (Hold hands with palms facing; clap three times)
Here are baby's soldiers, standing in a row.
   (Hold fingers straight)
Here is baby's trumpet. Toot-too, toot-too-too.
   (Pretend to blow with doubled fists to mouth)
Here is the way that baby plays at peek-a-boo.
   (Hands over eyes, then peek)
Here's a big umbrella to keep the baby dry.
   (Cup one hand over the upright finger of the
other hand)
Here is baby's cradle to rock the baby bye.
   (Cup hands together and rock)

Hands on Shoulders

Hands on shoulders, hands on knees,
Hand behind you, if you please;
Touch your shoulders, now your nose,
Now your hair and now your toes;
Hands up high in the air,
Down at your sides, now touch your hair;
Hands up high as before,
Now clap your hands: one, two, three, four.

Author unknown

Ten Little Fingers

I have ten little fingers,
And they all belong to me.
I can make them do things—
Would you like to see?

I can shut them up tight
Or open them out wide,
I can put them together
Or let them all hide.

I can make them jump high,
I can make them jump low,
I can lay them gently in my lap,
And leave them there just so.

Author unknown

Here Is a Beehive

Here is a beehive. (Make a beehive with fist)
Where are the bees? (Pretend to look around for
them)
Hiding inside (Try to see inside the beehive)
Where nobody sees.
Soon they'll come creeping (Unlock fist slowly)
Out of the hive.
One, two, three, four, five. (Extend fingers one at
a time)
BZZZZZZZZZZZ (Flutter hands all around as bees
flying)

Author unknown

Once I Saw a Little Bird

Once I saw a little bird
   Come hop, hop, hop'
So I cried, "Little bird,
   Will you stop , stop, stop?"

I was going to the window
   To say, "How do you do?"
But he shook his little tail,
   And far away he flew.

Author unknown

I Could Be an Airplane

I could be an airplane! (Hold arms out and soar)
  I could be a truck (Turn big steering wheel)
I could be a bi…g bird! (Hold arms out and flap wings)
  I could be a duck! (Tuck fingers into arm pits,
    stoop and "waddle" in a circle)

I could be a sailboat. (Touch fingertips overhead)
  I could be the sea. (Up/down wave motions with hands)
I could be a wha…le. (Extend both arms to show length)
  But, I'd rather be ME! Both hands on chest)

"I Could Be an Airplane" from BUSY BEING ME (Fitness, Fun and
Fundamentals) by Ruth I Dowell. © 1988. Published and distributed
by Pollyana Productions (P.O. Box 3222, Terre Haute, IN 47803).
Ruth is also the author of MOVE OVER, MOTHER GOOSE!

Kindness to Animals

Little children, never give
Pain to things that feel and live;
Let the gentle robin come
For the crumbs you save at home,—
As his meat you throw along
He'll repay you with a song
Never hurt the timid hare
Peeping from her green grass lair,
Let her come and sport and play
On the lawn at close of day;
The little lark goes soaring high
To the bright windows of the sky,
Singing as if 'twere always spring,
And fluttering on an untired wing—
Oh, let him sing his happy song,
Nor do these gentle creatures wrong.

Author unknown

May Day

Spring is coming, spring is coming,
  Birdies, build your nest;
Weave together straw and feather,
  Doing each your best.

Spring is coming spring is coming,
  Flowers are coming too;
Pansies, lilies, daffodillies,
  Now are coming through.

Spring is coming, spring is coming,
  All around is fair;
Shimmer and quiver on the river,
  Joy is everywhere.

Author unknown

Little Robin Red-Breast

Little Robin Red-breast sat upon a tree,
Up went Pussy-cat, and down went he;
Down came Pussy-cat, and away Robin ran;
Says little Robin Red-breast,
"Catch me if you can."

Little Robin Red-breast jumped upon a wall,
Pussy-cat jumped after him, and almost got a fall;
Little Robin chirped and sang,
And what did Pussy say?
Pussy-cat said "Mew," and Robin flew away.

Author unknown

The Squirrel

Whisky, frisky,
Hippity hop,
Up he goes
To the tree top!

Whirly, twirly
Round and round
Down he scampers
To the ground.

Furly, curly,
What a tail
Tall as a feather,
Broad as a sail!

Where's his supper?
In the shell,
Snappity, crackity,
Out it fell!

Author unknown

Catkin

I have a little pussy,
    And her coat is silver gray;
She lives in a great wide meadow
    And she never runs away.
She always is a pussy,
    She'll never be a cat
Because—she's a pussy willow!
    Now what do you think of that!

Author unknown

How They Sleep

Some things go to sleep in such a funny way:
Little birds stand on one leg and tuck their heads
    away;

Chickens do the same, standing on their perch;
Little mice lie soft and still, as they were in
    church

Kittens curl up close in such a funny ball;
Horses hang their sleepy heads and stand still in a
    stall;

Sometimes dogs stretch out, or curl up a heap;
Cows lie down upon their sides when they would
    go to sleep.

But little babies dear are snugly tucked in beds,
Warm with blankets all so soft, and pillows for
    their heads.

Bird and beast and babe—I wonder which of all
Dream the dearest dreams that down from dream-
    land fall!

Author unknown

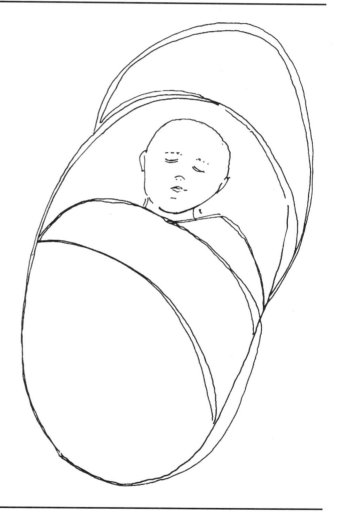

Buttons

The front ones I can button fine
The side ones keep me busy
But buttons all the way behind
I hunt until I'm dizzy!

Author unknown

Kite

I often sit and wish that I
Could be a kite up in the sky,
And ride upon the breeze and go
Whichever way I chanced to blow.

Author unknown

Taking Off

The airplane taxis down the field
And heads into the breeze,
It lifts its wheels above the ground,
It skims above the trees,
It rises high and higher
Away up toward the sun,
It's just a speck against the sky
—And now it's gone!

Author unknown

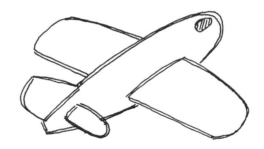

Falling Snow

See the pretty snowflakes
    Falling from the sky;
On the walk and housetop
    Soft and thick they lie.

On the window-ledges
    On the branches bare;
Now how fast they gather,
    Filling in the air.

Author unknown

The Secret

We have a secret, just we three,
The robin, and I, and the sweet cherry-tree;
The bird told the tree, and the tree told me,
And nobody knows it but just we three.

But of course the robin knows it best,
Because he built the—I shan't tell the rest;
And laid the four little—something in it—
I'm afraid I shall tell it every minute.

But if the tree and the robin don't peep,
I'll try my best the secret to keep;
Though I know when the little birds fly about
Then the whole secret will be out.

Author unknown

Friends

I like to play with many boys,
    But there's a special one,
For Andy is my truest friend:
We plan together days on end,
    And have a lot of fun.

We have our ups and downs, of course,
    And often disagree;
    Sometimes I let him have his way,
And sometimes in our work and play,
    He does the same for me.

For friends must give and friends must take,
And each must do his part to make
    A friendship tried and true.

Author unknown

Mr. Nobody

I know a funny little man,
 As quiet as a mouse,
Who does the mischief that is done
 In everybody's house!
There's no one ever sees his face,
 And yet we all agree
That every plate we break was cracked
 By Mr. Nobody.

'Tis he who always tears our books,
 Who leaves the door ajar,
He pulls the buttons from our shirts,
 And scatters pins afar;
That speaking door will always speak,
 For, prithee, don't you see,
We leave the oiling to be done
 By Mr. Nobody.

The fingermarks upon the door
 By none of us are made;
We never leave the blinds unclosed,
 To let the curtains fade.
The ink we never spill; the boots
 That lying round you see
Are not our boots—they all belong
 To Mr. Nobody.

Author unknown

Five Little Squirrels

Five little squirrels sat up in a tree.
The first one said, "What do I see?"
The second one said, "A man with a gun."
The third one said, "Then we'd better run."
The fourth one said, "Let's hide in the shade."
The fifth one said, "I'm not afraid."
Then BANG went the gun,
And how they did run.

Author unknown

Growing Up

My birthday is coming tomorrow,
And then I'm going to be four;
And I'm getting so big that already,
I can open the kitchen door;
I'm very much taller than Baby,
Though today I am only three;
And I'm bigger than Bob-tail the puppy,
Who used to be bigger than me.

Author unknown

White Sheep

White sheep, white sheep,
On a blue hill,
When the wind stops
You all stand still.
When the wind blows
You walk away slow.
White sheep, white sheep,
Where do you go?

Author unknown

Long, Long Ago

Windows through the olive trees
    Softly did blow,
Round little Bethehem
    Long, long ago.

Sheep on the hillside lay
    Whiter than snow;
Shepherds were watching them,
    Long, long ago.

Then from the happy sky,
    Angels bent low,
Singing their songs of joy,
    Long, long ago.

For in a manger bed,
    Cradled we know,
Christ came to Bethlehem.
    Long, long ago.

Author unknown

O, Look at the Moon

O, look at the moon,
    She is shining up there;
O, mother, she looks
    Like a lamp in the air.

Last week she was smaller,
    And shaped like a bow,
But now she's grown bigger,
    And round like an O.

Author unknown

The Big Clock

Slowly ticks the big clock;
Tick-tock, tick-tock!
But Cuckoo clock ticks double-quick;
Tick-a-tock-a, tick-a-tock-a,
Tick-a-tock-a, tick!

Author unknown

Good Friend

Good friend, good friend,
Turn around.

Good friend, good friend,
Touch the ground.

Good friend, good friend,
Reach up high.

Good friend, good friend,
Wink one eye.

Good friend, good friend,
Slap your knees.

Good friend, good friend,
Sit down, please.

Chapter 5

Games For Parties

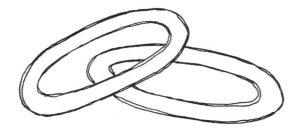

Ring Toss

Players stand behind a line marked with masking tape on the floor. They take turns throwing rings toward an object (legs of an upturned chair, stobs from a croquet set, a 6 inch dowel stick glued to a large piece of heavy cardboard).

Do not keep score. (All preschoolers want to be winners.) Praise each child as he makes a "ringer."

Musical Chairs

Gather enough chairs for each participant to be seated, less one chair. The chairs are placed in a row back to back. Use a piano or record player to provide the music. When the music begins, the preschoolers march in a line around the chairs. When the music stops, players hurry to sit down in a chair. The player without a chair may help the adult remove the chair for the next time. (Remember that preschoolers should not be called losers.)

The remaining players march again until the music stops. Then one more player and chair are removed. Repeat this procedure until the last chair is left or until the children lose interest.

(If the child remaining the longest is rewarded, everyone should be rewarded.)

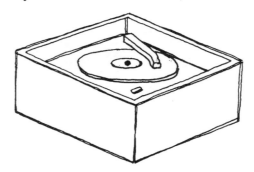

Drop the Handkerchief

Players join hands to form a circle and then drop hands. One child is selected to be "It." That child walks around the outside of the circle and drops the handkerchief behind one of the children. "It" runs around the circle with the person with the handkerchief chasing him. The object is for that person to catch "It" before "It" reaches the empty place. The chaser then becomes "It."

Bowling

Set up ten bowling pins (blocks, tall empty milk cartons, tall empty plastic soft-drink bottles) in a V-shaped arrangement. Players take turns rolling a ball from a designated line to try to knock down the bowling pins.

Squirrel and Nut

A child is chosen to be the squirrel and is given a nut to use during the game. The other children pretend to be sleeping (either standing or sitting) with one hand outstretched, palm open. The squirrel quietly makes his rounds, and drops the nut into someone's hand. That child jumps up and chases the squirrel, who is safe when he reaches his "nest" (tree, chair, some other designated spot). If the squirrel reaches his nest without being caught, he may choose someone to be the squirrel. If caught, the chaser becomes the squirrel.

What Color?

One child closes his eyes as another child has a piece of colored paper pinned on his back. When "It" opens his eyes, he tries to see the color on the other child's back. The child with the colored paper on his back moves around rapidly to keep "It" from seeing the color.

Doggy, Doggy, Where's Your Bone?

The children sit in a semicircle. One chair is placed in the center with its back to the group.

One child is selected to be the dog, and he sits in the chair. Underneath the chair is placed an object (eraser, crayon, block) to represent the dog's bone. The adult chooses someone to quietly tiptoe to get the bone and then that person hides it by sitting on it. The entire group says, "Doggy, doggy, where's your bone?" The "dog" then guesses who might have the bone hidden. (You may want to give just three guesses to hasten the process.) If the "dog" guesses correctly, the person hiding the bone becomes the dog or the dog may choose someone to be "It."

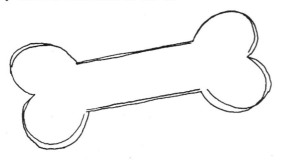

Button, Button—Who Has the Button?

Everyone sits in a circle with the palms of his hands pressed together. One child is "It" and is given a button or small object to press between the palm of his hands.

"It" walks around the circle from child-to-child pressing his hands between those of each child. He drops the button into the hands of one child although he continues all the way around the group trying to disguise where the button is. When he has gone around the circle, "It" chooses someone to guess who has the button.

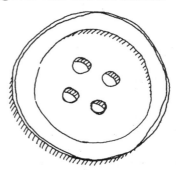

Drop the Clothespins

Gather several milk cartons, wash them thoroughly, and cut off the tops. Gather clothespins to let the preschoolers take turns trying to drop the clothespins into the carton. Each child may have eight or ten clothespins at a time. (You will need only one milk carton if there are only a few children.)

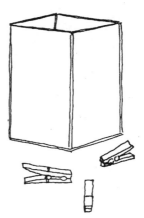

Singing Game

Look at the Musical Games chapter in this book to choose one or two singing games to play.

Guess What

Choose one person to be "It." "It" goes out of the room. The remaining children decide upon some object in the room to be a mystery object. When "It" returns to the room, she calls on someone to give a hint about the object such as "It is on a table." Each child called on gives some clue. The last one to give a hint becomes "It," or that person may choose someone to be "It."

Mother Hen

One child is chosen to be the Mother Hen, and the other children represent her chicks. Mother Hen is blindfolded, and she waits for the chicks to hide. When Mother Hen says, "Cluck, cluck" calling her baby chicks, the chicks MUST respond, "Peep, peep." The last chick to be found may become the Mother Hen or that person may choose someone to be the Mother Hen.

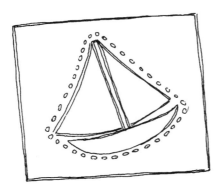

Sewing Cards

Purchase a set of simple sewing cards (or make a set using poster board and a hole puncher). Provide a plastic needle for each child, along with pieces of yarn. Ask the children to sew "in and out" of the holes to make their pictures. This item may be taken home as a favor.

A Fun Board

Make a fun board by putting together a 1-inch wooden board (approximately 10 feet long and 10 inches wide) and two 4-by-4s (approximately 18-24 inches long).

Place the plank on the 4-by-4 supports, centered, and extending 6 to 10 inches beyond the supports. Ask a child to jump up and down in the center. If the plank hits the floor as he jumps, stiffen the board by moving the supports toward the center. When the "give" of the board is adjusted, bolt the three pieces together.

Suggest different kinds of activities to do on the board:

• Jump forward; jump backward; jump sideways (to the right, to the left with feet together).

• Hop forward on the right foot, on the left foot; hop backward; hop forward five hops; hop in place five times.

• Jump in place; jump six times and jump off; count your jumps; clap your hands as you jump; clap your hands on every other jump.

• Jump in the center of the board facing a partner; jump in the center and bounce a ball on the floor.

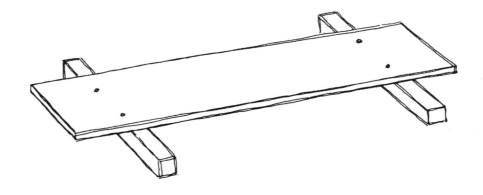

Parachute Fun

Provide a colorful sheet for this activity. If it is an old sheet, cut it to make it round. Find some open space and spread out the sheet (parachute). The children gather around the parachute and take hold of the edges. Each child pulls on the parachute to stretch it tightly.

First, tell the children to walk around in a circle holding the parachute, keeping it stretched tightly. You may use a drum or some other instrument to give the speed for walking, even up to a running tempo.

Try variations, such as having the children hold the parachute high to let a child run under it. Another variation is to try to balance a beach ball or balloon on the parachute.

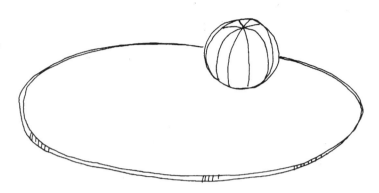

Balloon Toss

Provide several round, inflated balloons in case one bursts.

Guide the preschoolers to form a circle holding hands. They stand close to each other and then drop hands. Choose two children to stand inside the circle. Toss a balloon into the air inside the circle. The two children try to keep it up in the air inside the circle. If the balloon falls to the ground, these two choose two others to take their places inside the circle, and they join the other children in forming the circle.

Blowing Bubbles

Provide each child a homemade "blower" to participate in the fun of blowing bubbles. This solution makes bubbles: 2 cups water, 1 to 2 tablespoons liquid soap, 1/4 cup glycerine. Mix ingredients thoroughly. To prepare a "blower" for each child, use a Styrofoam cup into which a small hole is punched about one inch from the bottom. Each child also needs a drinking straw to place into the hole.

Each child dips the open end of her cup into the bubble solution. With the cup upside down, she blows gently into the straw. (If the cups are held upright, the bubbles will not be as large.)

Mine Are Gone

Gather bits of Styrofoam packing pieces or use small square pieces of construction paper. Save produce trays until you have enough for each child to have one. Prepare a poster board divided into five sections with one large numeral from 1-5 written in each section. Use a beanbag to toss onto the poster board.

Each child begins with a tray and 20 pieces of Styrofoam. A child tosses the beanbag onto the poster. The number on which the beanbag lands is the number of Styrofoam pieces the child removes from his tray. The player who empties his tray first says loudly, "Mine are gone."

Leader of the Group

Choose one child to be "It." That child leaves the room while the other boys and girls in the circle choose one person to be the leader. (An adult may be the leader first to set the pace.)

When "It" returns, the leader starts some motion (clapping hands, swinging the foot, snapping fingers) and the other children imitate immediately. Caution the children to watch other people in addition to glancing at the leader. As the children engage in these activities, "It" tries to determine who is the leader.

Viewing Slides

It is thrilling for boys and girls to see themselves on a screen.

Before the party, ask the mothers of the invited guests for colored slides or movies of their children. Show these pictures at a time when the boys and girls need a rest.

Toy Swap

Ask each child to bring to the party an old toy (in good condition) placed in a paper bag and tied with a ribbon. While the honoree opens his gifts, suggest that each child gets to choose a paper bag with a toy inside to take home.

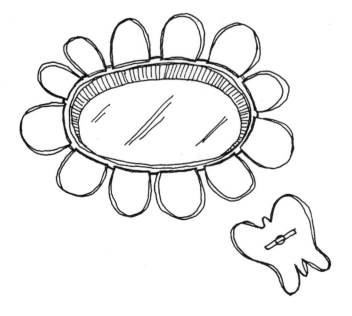

Butterfly Toss

Decorate a disposable pie pan to look like a flower. Fasten construction paper petals around the rim of the pan.

Each child gets a butterfly (about six inches across the wings) cut from construction paper. First, the preschoolers decorate their butterflies, then tape a penny to the underside to serve as a weight.

When ready to play, place the "flower" in the middle of the table or floor. The children take turns standing behind a line to toss their butterflies toward the flower.

Roll Under the Bridge

To make a bridge use two tall tin cans of the same size or use two tall blocks. Place a book or a long block on top to make a bridge.

With masking tape, mark the starting line about six feet from the bridge. Give each player two chances to roll a small ball under the bridge. (If the group is large, make two or more bridges to shorten the waiting time.)

Bat the Ball

To make a bat for each child, bend a coat hanger into a diamond shape. Pull an old nylon stocking over the hanger and knot it at each end.

Go outside and give each child an inflated balloon and a bat. Allow the children to play as they wish with the balloons and bats. They may try batting the balloons to one another. If possible, provide extra balloons to replace the ones that burst.

Roll the Ball

Provide each participant with a ball of similar size such as a tennis ball. Mark each ball a different color for a child to identify his. To begin the game, each player rolls his ball on the grass (or floor if indoors). Then instruct each player to take a turn trying to roll his ball so that it will hit some of the other balls. Keep score in the following way:

Hit one ball—5 points
Hit two balls—10 points
Hit three balls—15 points

As long as a player continues to hit other balls, he keeps on rolling his ball. He is not to hit any ball twice until he hits another ball.

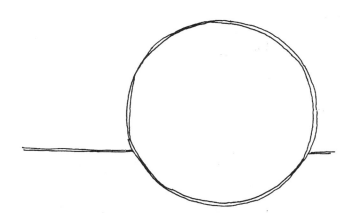

Cluck! Cluck!

The boys and girls form a circle. One person is selected to be "It." That person is blindfolded and given a ruler, a stick, or a closed umbrella as a pointer. "It" stands in the center of the circle while the children catch hands and walk around him. Everyone stops when "It" taps loudly on the floor or ground.

"It" points the umbrella at someone. That person says, "Cluck, cluck." The blindfolded person tries to guess who it is. If he guesses correctly, he trades places with the player. If he guesses incorrectly, they march around again. (If the participants are young or have difficulty guessing, give "It" three guesses.)

Penny Toss

You need five pennies for each child and an empty oatmeal box or coffee can to play this game.

Using masking tape, mark a line designating where a preschooler is to stand to toss his pennies into the box or can. The preschoolers take turns trying to toss their five pennies into the box. To make the game more challenging, move the box a little farther from the marked line for pitching.

Applaud the winner. If you give surprises, everyone is included. (It is difficult for preschoolers to lose; everyone wants to be a winner at this age.)

Story Time

Invite an adult who is good at telling preschool stories to come to the party. Ask that person to be prepared to tell a short, interesting story.

Sock Race

Divide the group into two teams. If it is a small group (less than eight), it can be fun just watching each other run in this special way.

Each child runs while holding onto the tops of his socks.

Stoop

This is a game of following directions, rather than following the leader. The adult stoops saying, "I say, stoop." The adult stands saying, "I say, stand." Occasionally, the leader stoops when he says *stand* or vice versa. Remind the preschoolers that they are to do what you say rather than what you do, so they must listen carefully.

After playing for a while, suggest that the children who make the wrong movement will sit down. Who is last to stand?

Sometimes I'm Tall, Sometimes I'm Small

Choose one child to be "It." She stands with her back to the group and closes her eyes. The group chants and acts out the following:

Sometimes I'm very, very small,
Sometimes I'm very, very tall.
Sometimes small,
Sometimes tall.
Guess what I am now.

As the group says the last line, they either stay tall or become small. If "It" guesses correctly, she chooses someone else to take her place.

Over the Water

Lead the children to form a circle. Choose one child to be "It." That child stands in the center of the circle. The other children join hands and walk around the circle as they chant:

Jason over the water, Jason over the sea.
Jason caught a blackbird, but he can't catch me.

The children in the circle immediately stoop. "It" tries to touch a child before he can get in a stooping position. The child who is caught becomes "It."

Peanut Hunt

Hide a number of peanuts in the room or outdoors. Designate the time for the children to begin hunting for peanuts. The one who finds the most peanuts is applauded.

It is a good learning experience to be able to count the peanuts found.

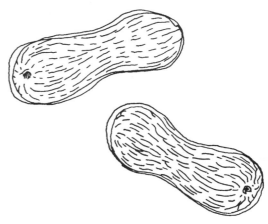

Happy Birthday

Choose one child to sit in a chair with her back to the group and eyes closed. Select another child to tiptoe behind "It" and say, "Happy birthday." "It" has three guesses to determine the person who spoke. If the child guesses correctly, the other person becomes "It." However, if "It" has difficulty guessing correctly, after a couple of times, choose another person to be "It."

A Spanish Game

Preschoolers join hands and form a circle. As they walk around, they chant:

To the wheel of the *chuchurumble* [choo-choo-room-BEHL]
Passes a cart full of honey.
Hard bread, tender bread,
Let (child's name) turn her head.

Rather than turn the head only, the child turns around completely and continues walking around the circle facing outward. The game continues until all the preschoolers are facing the other way.

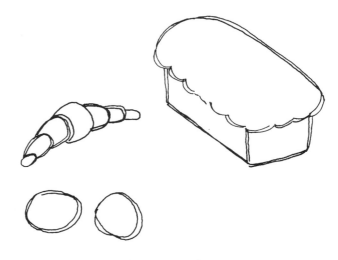

Cat, Cat, Catch the Rat

Ask the boys and girls to join hands to form a circle. Choose one child to be "It." "It" walks around the outside of the circle. "It" stops between two children, touches their arms, and says, "Cat, cat, catch the rat." One child runs one way, and the other child runs in the opposite direction. Both seek to return to "It" first because the first player to touch "It's" arm becomes the next "It."

Take Away One

Place several object (things associated with birthdays, nature items, pictures, etc.) on a large tray for all of the children to see. One child closes his eyes while the adult (or child) removes one item from the tray. When all of the children say, "Take away one," the person with eyes closed opens them and tries to name the item that was taken away. Repeat the procedure as others take a turn.

Run for Your Life

Divide the group into two teams. Each team forms a straight line, one person behind the other.

The first person in line on each team is given a tablespoon with a cotton ball in it. The player is to run to a designated spot (around a tree, around a chair, around a person), return, and hand the spoon with the cotton ball to the next participant. If the cotton ball falls out of the spoon, the player must hurriedly pick it up, replace it in the spoon, and continue the race.

All can clap for the team that finishes first. With preschoolers do not emphasize winning and losing as everyone strongly yearns to be the winner. If rewards are given, everyone gets a reward.